How to Be Aware of Principles, Patterns, and Promises

Bee Devotionals By Sheila Textor

Independently published by Bee Ministries.
Blytheville, Arkansas

ISBN: 979-8-9887297-1-6

All scriptures used in this devotional come from the King James Version of the Bible, which exists in the public domain in the United States.

Interior art designed for Bee Ministries by Victoria Neal @victorianeal2001.

Check out Sheila's other works on Amazon:
Life After the Mistake
How to Bee Prosperous
How to Be Intentional With Your Words
How to Be Healthy, Wealthy, and Wise
How to Be Prayerful, Powerful, and Purposeful
How to Believe in Your Dreams
How to Be Courageous
How to Be Fruitful, Fat, and Flourishing
ebook: *How to Be a Writer*

Find Sheila on YouTube at Bee Ministries
Facebook @LifeAfterTheMistake

How to Be Aware of Principles, Patterns, and Promises

By Sheila Textor

Contents

Part 1: Principles

Part 2: Patterns

Part 3: Promises

Introduction

I have found that the Bible consists of three main attributes: Principles, Patterns, and Promises. You can't address principles without Proverbs coming to your mind. There are principles for living, giving, and just about everything that pertains to this life on earth. With those principles, you will see patterns that bring about the promises of God.

One of the greatest principles I have found in the Bible is being thankful. God speaks on this subject over and over. We create a pattern of thankfulness by doing it consistently for all things. When we are thankful, it brings joy to our spirit and healing to our minds. It releases chemicals in our bodies and works like medicine. It can lower blood pressure and heart rate and help with overall relaxation (Health benefits of gratitude - UCLA Health). We can clearly see the principle, pattern, and promise of being thankful.

The Bible is not a storybook to entertain us. It's a book with instructions, examples, ups and downs, and ins and outs. It's truly a life-giving book we can apply to every area of our lives.

I hope you enjoy this devotional as much as I have enjoyed writing it. Whether you read one a day or consume all 31 days in one setting, it will encourage you to keep moving forward in this thing called life. Nobody gets a free ride. If you live any length of time, you will find the 3 Ps (principles, patterns, and promises) in your journey. It's up to us to choose wisely so that our lives will be filled with the promises of God.

By no means does this devotional cover every principle, pattern, or promise. These are just a few that have stood out to me over the years as a part of my Christian walk. May God bless you as you read each reflection and write your thoughts on the journal pages provided.

Thank you from the bottom of my heart for supporting this ministry and helping another fellow laborer in the Kingdom of God to fulfill their purpose and call.

-Sheila

Part I
Principles

Day 1

Commit thy works unto the LORD, and thy thoughts shall be established.

Proverbs 16:3

Being committed is a principle. No matter what we set out to do, the first thing we must consider is whether we will be committed. We can see all three attributes in this one verse. Commit our work to the Lord, then our thoughts (patterns) shall be established (promises).

Prayer has to be a principle in our life. Reading the Word of God, faithfulness, and discipline are all connected to principles.

Commitment is not popular. It requires accountability. It requires us to show up. When we truly get committed to the things of God, we will find it much easier to show up. Show up for our church. Show up for our families. Show up for the lost. Show up for ourselves. Yes, even for ourselves. Nobody will know that you are not giving your best at first. That is why we should push past our own passiveness. This principle of commitment can make you or break you. You must be committed to your dreams, goals, and desires. Nobody can put in the work for you. Sure, others can help, but only you can fulfill the call in your life. What work are you committed to today? Let commitment be one principle that will move your life's gauge.

Prayer (speak aloud)

Dear Lord, help me to stay committed to the work. This one principle is so vital to my life as a whole. Show me how to use it to stay focused on where You are leading me. My life is in Your hands. Every prayer is dipped in hope. I want to commit my thoughts to You. I want to commit my work to You. Please teach me how to show up for my own growth. I can't help others if I'm not investing in being committed. I don't want to just appear that I'm all in. I want to be true to others. You are the only one who truly knows where I am. You know my heart. You know my thoughts. I can get easily distracted and fall short of the work You have called me to do. Please help me pour my life into kingdom work, no matter what that may look like for me. Amen.

What is one thing that you struggle with staying committed to?
Why do you feel you fall short in that area?

_____

_____

_____

_____

_____

_____

_____

_____

_____

_____

_____

_____

_____

_____

_____

_____

_____

_____

_____

_____

_____

Day 2

When a man's ways please the LORD, he maketh even his enemies to be at peace with him.

Proverbs 16:7

Pleasing the Lord. What a powerful principle! I don't always do it perfectly. What about you?

I don't pray like I need to. I definitely don't fast as I should. Even though I read a lot, I should do more deep study. Yes, I just shared some of my faults with you. Even at our best, this ole flesh doesn't measure up sometimes. I just convicted myself, but I'm going to do better. I want my enemies to be at peace with me. When peace is lacking, the devil jumps on the bandwagon, which adds even more chaos. Psalms 34:14 tells us to pursue peace.

What does pleasing the Lord look like for us? Here are a few ways we can please the Lord. Treat others the way we want to be treated. Show love when love is not deserved. Do good to them that use you. Do good to those who are speaking all manner of evil against you. Matthew 5 tells us we are blessed when we are persecuted. The list is endless. Our ways should please the Lord.

Prayer (speak aloud)

Heavenly Father, let my ways please You. Teach me what that looks like from Your perspective. Help me to bring this flesh under Your rule. I don't like to think about enemies, but we all have them. Number one is Satan. Please help me to recognize his tactics. He has to have a vessel to work through, just like You. I don't want to make myself an easy target for him. I don't want to be available for him. I will seek Your ways so I can have peace with those who oppose me. This is an important principle to live by. It doesn't always come easy, but Your Word is our instruction manual to help us please You. Thank You for making even my enemies at peace with me. Amen.

What are some ways that you can please the Lord? Which one do you struggle with the most?

Day 3

**Pleasant words are as an honeycomb, sweet to
the soul, and health to the bones.**

Proverbs 16:24

Words, words, words. It's no secret that speaking the right words ranks high on the list of principles — I would say it's the main one. The Bible doesn't mince words about the importance of our words. They matter so much that life and death are in them. This scripture gives us an almost unmatched comparison.

The honeycomb is where the bees store their honey. It's full of sweetness that refreshes our souls. Words are like medicine. Healing hearts. Healing minds. They are even healing to our bones. Words are powerful. They can destroy something in minutes or bring life in one breath. The words we use daily will show up in our lives. If we continue to use negative words, our lives will reflect that. It's hard not to express patterns in this verse as well. All three of the P's are in this one verse. We can see the principle, the pattern, and the promise. My dear readers, God orchestrated the Bible so profoundly. We stand in awe at the wise applications that we use every day. He doesn't leave us to wander from day to day. He gave us the Bible.

Prayer (speak aloud)

Thank You, God, for giving us Your Word. Through Your Word, we can know the principles that build our lives. I want wholesome words to flow from my mouth. I want words that edify and not tear down. Through words, battles are won or lost. Let my words be encouraging to those that are discouraged. Let them be a comfort to those who are grieving. Let them praise You during the storm. Help me, dear Lord, always consider myself when speaking to others and use pleasant words. I never want to hurt my witness with empty words. I never want to cause others to stumble because I was unwise with something so precious yet powerful. My words, oh God, are my testimony. Amen.

Do you struggle with your words?
Does it come naturally to use your words wisely or do you have to be extra careful?

I have to be extra careful!

_____

_____

_____

_____

_____

_____

_____

_____

_____

_____

_____

_____

_____

_____

_____

_____

_____

_____

_____

_____

Day 4

Giving thanks always for all things unto God and the Father in the name of our Lord Jesus Christ;

Ephesians 5:20

Being thankful would come in second on the principle scale. *Always* is a strong word in our vocabulary. This is one of those principles that can be easy at times. We can be thankful when our bills are paid. Thankful when we have good jobs and money in the bank. Thankful when our marriage is great, or our children are doing good. Thankful that the book we wrote is helping thousands of people. Insert some things you are grateful for.

Then there are those not-so-great things. Delay, divorce, and a hundred other things that are not working out. I'm there now. Things are moving slowly. Slow in our remodel (we are remodeling our house). Slow in book sales. Slow in moving forward. Being thankful no matter what is going on has brought so much peace. That is why it's so powerful. When we are thankful during confusion and chaos, we confuse the enemy. I give thanks for the roof over my head daily. I give thanks for our food, a bed to sleep in, a good husband, and my health. 1 Thess. 5:18 says, "In every thing give thanks: for this is the will of God in Christ Jesus concerning you."

Prayer (speak aloud)

Thank You, Heavenly Father, for teaching me to be thankful. I know that through this simple act of obedience, my circumstances can change. You showed me over and over through the Word that being thankful was an excellent way to stay in peace. Thank You for healing my soul and mind. Thank You for mercy and grace. Thank You for showing me that being thankful is a healing balm. You have shown me that being thankful is one of Your principles for achieving greater heights in my walk with You. I want to always show gratitude toward others. With Your help, I can honor my friends and even my spouse. When I honor another person, I am showing my gratitude for them. This is Your will for my life. Amen.

Do you feel thankful in all circumstances?
Do you struggle with being a thankful person?
Write a list of things that you are thankful for.

_____
_____
_____
_____
_____
_____
_____
_____
_____
_____
_____
_____
_____
_____
_____
_____
_____
_____
_____
_____
_____
_____
_____

Day 5

My son, attend to my words; incline thine ear unto my sayings. Let them not depart from thine eyes; keep them in the midst of thine heart. For they are life unto those that find them, and health to all their flesh.

Proverbs 4:20-22

The principle of getting the Word in your heart, letting it not depart from thine eyes, is like finding the fountain of youth. Scriptures like Psalm 103:5 KJV, "Who satisfieth thy mouth with good things; so that thy youth is renewed like the eagle's.", help you to see the amazing benefit of attending to God's Word. The Word has life. It breathes into our circumstances. It lifts us up, encourages us, and calms our chaos. It heals our physical bodies as well as our brokenness. If anything would be the heartbeat of God, I believe His Word would be at the top of the list.

Many battles were won in the Bible by simply knowing the Word. Many people were saved by hearing it and applying it to their lives. Verse 22 says they are life to those who find them. We must diligently seek out what the Bible says about different areas of our lives. Hosea 4:6 puts this principle about the Word into one concept, my people are destroyed for lack of knowledge. We must know the Word. It's crucial to our existence.

Prayer (speak aloud)

Oh God, how loving and kind You are to give me a remedy to all my life's situations. You didn't leave me without an answer. You lift me daily through the Word. Please help me to make the time to attend to thy Word. Help me to put it before my eyes and to put it in my heart. Your Word has healed many areas in my life. I thank You for teaching me the principle of Your Word. I have the answer to many questions by simply opening the Bible and asking You to speak to me through it. I can do all things through You because You strengthen me. I am the head and not the tail. Why? Because Your Word tells me I am. I can stand in a fiery trial. I can go through deep waters. I can go through the fire. I can give You praise because Your Word is in my heart. Amen.

Do you always go to the Word when life gets hard?
Will you be more intentional with putting His Word in your heart?
Write some of your favorite scriptures and meditate on them today.

Day 6

Keep thy heart with all diligence; for out of it are the issues of life.

Proverbs 4:23

The Bible repeatedly mentions the heart. Decisions and actions flow from this area, which is why God tells us to guard it with all diligence. Bitterness will grow there, and anger will linger. Envy and strife can be traced back to the heart—not the blood-pumping one, the one that holds your thoughts, the one that tries to tell you you can't make it. It's called the spirit man.

Reigning in that part of us is a principle that God desperately wants us to learn. The principle of the heart is that everything flows from it. Let us not just focus on the negative side of it, but we can also point out the positive side. When we have joy in our hearts, it shows. When we have peace in our hearts, it shows. The main principle about the heart is that your whole life can hang in the balance naturally and spiritually.

One passage in the Bible reveals that the biggest problem with the heart is that it is desperately wicked. It's the fleshly man who wants to rise up and dominate. Just like the tongue, no man can tame it. We can't fix our hearts. It takes the spirit of God working with us to get it to that good place. Even then, it's a daily discipline. We can't make it without God leading us and guiding us in this area called the heart.

Prayer (speak aloud)

God, You tell us that the heart of man is full of evil. You have given us a way of escape from this evil. God, You made it plain that we can't fix this problem alone. Please help me to guard it according to Your Word. When You said the heart of man is desperately wicked, You were letting us know how detrimental it could be to our souls without Your help. Help me to not allow bitterness, unforgiveness, or strive to take up residence in my heart. Help me to keep my heart with all diligence (intentional effort). When I allow my heart to rule, let it be from a place of Biblical truth and pure love for others. Thank You for teaching me the important principle of my heart. I will pray that the fruit of the spirit will always be what flows from it. Amen.

What area do you struggle the most with?
What are the steps you will take in guarding your heart?

_____

_____

_____

_____

_____

_____

_____

_____

_____

_____

_____

_____

_____

_____

_____

_____

_____

_____

_____

_____

Day 7

Wisdom is the principal thing; therefore get wisdom: and with all thy getting get understanding. Exalt her, and she shall promote thee: she shall bring thee to honour, when thou dost embrace her. She shall give to thine head an ornament of grace: a crown of glory shall she deliver to thee.

Proverbs 4:7-9

Wisdom is another principle. Wisdom, knowledge, and understanding fall under the same umbrella but differ slightly. For today's devotional, we will hone in on wisdom. I love how the scripture refers to wisdom as her. Women, for the most part, are nurturers by nature. They are givers and encouragers.

When we allow wisdom to be number one in our lives, it will show up in every area. It doesn't just come. It is something we have to embrace. To embrace something means to make it a part of our life. When we have wisdom, it will promote our journey. It will bring honor. Through wisdom, grace will be like an ornament about you. In other words, it will be obvious to your friends and people in general that you move forward with wisdom in the forefront.

Wisdom is a rare commodity these days. People do whatever feels good at the moment with no thought of the consequences. Wisdom will cause you to seek God for answers. Wisdom will whisper at times and shout the next. Seek wisdom like life depends on it because, indeed, it does.

Prayer (speak aloud)

God, You are so mindful of us to give us these powerful truths. Please help me to let wisdom rule and reign in my life. Not the world's wisdom. The world says to get all you can at all costs. You tell us to use wisdom in all our choices. I need the wisdom that comes from above. I will seek You for answers to my life. When wisdom whispers no, I will hear her. When she shouts, I won't ignore her. How much plainer could You have spoken to me about wisdom being a principle. You gave us all the resources we needed in the very first line. When I seek wisdom, I'm going to do what is right. When I make wisdom one of the most essential principles in my life, I will have all I need to keep moving forward. Amen.

What situations do you need God's wisdom to move forward in?

_____

_____

_____

_____

_____

_____

_____

_____

_____

_____

_____

_____

_____

_____

_____

_____

_____

_____

_____

_____

_____

_____

Day 8

And thou shalt love the Lord thy God with
all thy heart, and with all thy soul, and with
all thy mind, and with all thy strength: this is
the first commandment.

Mark 12:30

Love has to be one of the strongest emotions that we can feel. It can also cause you the most heartache. What would life be like without love?

Love is an action word. love is a principle that will tear down walls and build bridges to help others. Love will turn the hardest heart. Love will show kindness, mercy, and grace to others. Our greatest love has to be toward God. Thou shalt, not thou maybe, love the Lord with all thine heart, soul, and strength. When we do this, we will put God first. We will put others first. We will sacrifice our own comfort for others. Why? Because that's what love does.

In the world we live in now, love is scarce. Yet, without it, life is meaningless. God loves us. He allowed Jesus to die on the cross to show His love. That is a selfless action. He didn't have to redeem us. He loved us, and He proved it.

Prayer (speak aloud)

Thank You, Lord, for loving me. You redeemed me with Your love. You showed me that love conquers all. Your Word says if we love You, we will keep Your commandments. Your commandments are not grievous. I have learned that putting love as a principle thing in my life will keep trouble at bay. Loving You with all my heart, soul, and strength has been the foundation on which I built everything else. Yes, love hurts sometimes. You chastise us because You love us. Just like we correct our children, even those who are grown or still at home because we love them. I'm thankful for the principle called love. Amen.

What does love look like for you? Do you feel like you love the way the Bible teaches us to?
I will be honest: sometimes, love is a hard pill to swallow when you want revenge.

_____

_____

_____

_____

_____

_____

_____

_____

_____

_____

_____

_____

_____

_____

_____

_____

_____

_____

_____

_____

_____

_____

_____

Day 9

Finally, my brethren, be strong in the Lord, and in the power of his might. Put on the whole armour of God, that ye may be able to stand against the wiles of the devil.

Ephesians 6:10-11

We can't talk about principles without sharing these foundational scriptures. Being strong in your faith walk is a must. Even on our best days, we need to be covered. Covered with the whole armour of God. Now, there are patterns in this passage as well. The pattern would be to put it on daily. We are expressing the principle of having it on. I would say let's keep it on 24/7. The devil doesn't sleep. He will try to invade your dreams and put all kinds of scenarios in your mind to cause you to fret and worry.

Each piece of armour has its purpose. Whenever God has put something in the Bible, it has great significance. We put this armour on by praying, reading, and studying God's Word. Not just occasionally, not just when we see trouble coming. We need it on at all times. It won't stop the attacks or the arrows from coming. What it will do is lessen the blows and protect our peace. Just don't turn your back. Satan fights dirty.

Prayer (speak aloud)

God, Your armour has been my protection many times. Forgive me for the times that I didn't have it on. If I'm knocked down by Satan, it's not Your fault. You have given me the principle of putting on the armour. I need it every day. I face the fiery darts daily. I have to guard my heart and mind at all times. I know that the enemy watches me, hoping that I will let down my shield. He hopes I will bend to his pressure and listen to the negative things he tries to put in my mind. He never sleeps. This is why we need the whole armour of God. We are not fighting flesh and blood. We are fighting wickedness in high places. We are fighting an unseen enemy. Thank You for giving us these life-saving principles to live victorious lives. Amen.

**Which part of the armour do you need the most?
Please read all the verses about each piece and what
there purpose is.**

_____
_____
_____
_____
_____
_____
_____
_____
_____
_____
_____
_____
_____
_____
_____
_____
_____
_____
_____
_____
_____
_____
_____
_____

Day 10

I know thy works: behold, I have set before thee an open door, and no man can shut it: for thou hast a little strength, and hast kept my word, and hast not denied my name.

Revelation 3:8

I want to use this last reflection to share a different insight on principles. God uses principles throughout His Word to teach us. They are guidelines to help us maneuver through our everyday lives. There are principles about money, health, and everything in between. But sometimes, God moves past principles when we need divine intervention.

This verse is about doors. The Bible refers to doors a lot in other places, but I chose this verse because it shows God stepping out of the normal way of opening doors. A door will usually have a lock. If it's locked, we will need the key. The principle of a locked door is to use a key to open it. When God wants to open a door in our life, He doesn't need a key. He simply opens the door for us to go in.

We are comparing natural doors to spiritual doors. God's key isn't like our key. He says for it to open and no man can shut it. Our key in the spirit is to keep His Word and don't deny His name. My desire is for you to know that God can overturn principles when we need Him to show up miraculously. We need the principles God has laid out to succeed in our endeavors. Never limit an unlimited God with our human reasoning. We will go from here to learning the patterns for understanding His principles.

Prayer (speak aloud)

God, I thank You for showing me Bible principles that will help me grow in wisdom, make good, sound decisions, and grow in the areas I need to. I'm also glad that when I need you to step out of the norm and open a door for me, You will do that. Thank You for showing me that if I follow the principles in Your Word, I can have a more stable life and be wiser in my choices. You have told me to be wise with my giving. In doing so, I can reap a harvest. I've stood on the principles of taking care of my body. You told me to be slow to speak and quick to hear. There is not one principle in the Bible that has not helped me in my walk with You. I thank You that no matter what I'm facing, You have a remedy laid out for me. You call them principles. Amen.

**Has God ever miraculously shown up for you?
Has He ever set His principles aside and moved for you?
He has for me many times.**

_____
_____
_____
_____
_____
_____
_____
_____
_____
_____
_____
_____
_____
_____
_____
_____
_____
_____
_____
_____

Part 2
Patterns

Day 11

So God created man in his own image, in the image of God created he him; male and female created he them. And God blessed them, and God said unto them, Be fruitful, and multiply, and replenish the earth, and subdue it: and have dominion over the fish of the sea, and over the fowl of the air, and over every living thing that moveth upon the earth.

Genesis 1:27-28

These two verses clearly show the pattern God lined up for us. He created male and female. He didn't just bless them; he also laid out the pattern for their lives. Be fruitful, multiply, and replenish the earth. I believe he was giving them the plan for children. Through this commandment, we have billions of people on the earth. This was a pattern for the future generations. We are to have dominion over the fish, the fowl, and every living creature. We, as God's people, should dominate.

The Word says we can be fruitful and flourish in old age. We must see the spiritual side of these scriptures as well. God wants us to bear fruit, not just once. Remember, our spiritual fruit is not for our life; it's for others to be nourished as well. Let's be fruitful. Let's multiply our gifts so that we can be part of God's grander plan.

Prayer (speak aloud)

God, You created me in Your image. You created me to mirror You and Your plan for my life. I will be fruitful. I will multiply in my gifts. Thank You for the pattern You laid out for me. Please help me to be the light You want me to be. You spoke into my future with Your Word so I could thrive and have dominion over situations that will arise. Animals are just a small part of my daily life. I see the pattern that You are conveying to me. Because of my human side, I understand the instructions in this passage. Thank You for getting on my level in the scriptures so I can take these patterns and live a fulfilled life. Your plan for my life is so much greater than I could imagine. For that, I am so thankful. Amen.

What other patterns do you see in these verses?
Do you feel like you dominate in life?
Write about areas that you need help with.

Day 12

Therefore shall a man leave his father and his mother, and shall cleave unto his wife: and they shall be one flesh.

Genesis 2:24

This pattern has been a hard one for many people to follow. We all know most marital problems stem from connected families. Although there are other areas, we will share this one today because it's highlighted in this verse. God knew if we didn't cut strings with our parents, it could cause problems. We don't have to cut them out of our life. We must cleave to our spouse and honor our marriage by honoring each other. When this pattern is not followed, it can cause more trouble and heartache than necessary. We need our families. We need support in our marriages from our parents and other loved ones. There has to be an understanding of what that looks like. How will that play out in the end?

The pattern is to become one, support one another, and love even when it's difficult. There are no perfect marriages, and no better way than the other. Each couple has to find that happy medium and work through it. I'm no expert on this subject. Even after 20 years, every day is a learning process for me. Following this pattern is challenging. We must pray for God to help us.

Prayer (speak aloud)

Dear Father, some of Your patterns are hard to follow. We know that behind every hard instruction, the results are for our good. Please help me to cleave to my spouse. Please help me honor and respect their views and decisions. To those who are not married at this time, allow them to take this to heart and let them be ready if and when they decide to become one with someone else. God, I love my parents. I never want to disrespect them. Help me to know when to draw the line if what they are saying or doing is causing a strain on my marriage. You gave me this pattern so that my future could become what You intended it to be. I will look to You for guidance and help when I face these situations. This is Your plan, not mine. Amen.

Do you and your spouse struggle in this area? If so, write about how you will work to follow this pattern from now on. If you don't, write about how you make it work. If you are not married, use this time to write about how you want this pattern to be right in your future.

_____

_____

_____

_____

_____

_____

_____

_____

_____

_____

_____

_____

_____

_____

_____

_____

_____

_____

_____

_____

_____

_____

_____

_____

Day 13

In every thing give thanks: for this is the will of God in Christ Jesus concerning you.

1 Thessalonians 5:18

The pattern of being thankful has to be one of the most beautiful and wonderful things that God has taught us. Why? The benefits of being thankful are inspiring. Eph. 5:20 tells us to give thanks always for all things. I have used these scriptures in the other devotionals because they are staple passages for us as Christians. Giving thanks is not just a cliche. God didn't give us this pattern so we feel good about ourselves or make others feel good. Although we do feel good about it, there is a spiritual side to being thankful.

Because it is one of God's instructions, there are spiritual benefits. We grow in trusting Him. We grow in our faith. We learn to look for better outcomes. Is this an easy pattern? No, sometimes it's not. We don't thank Him for a disease. We don't thank Him if our marriage is failing. We don't thank Him for the death of a loved one that was taken too soon. We must find something in that hard thing to thank Him for. I always say if living for God was easy, everyone would be doing it. If being Christ-like was easy, there would be no sinners. Let's thank Him today for redemption. Thank Him for the cross. Thank Him for loving us. He didn't leave us without a remedy.

Prayer (speak aloud)

God, I will start this prayer by simply saying thank you. Thank You for the easy times. Thank You for the blessings. I have a home. I have food on my table. I have my health. I have a good husband. I know that everyone cannot pray this prayer. I pray that whoever is praying that they can find an area to be thankful. My most repeated prayer is I will be thankful for the good, the bad, and the ugly. I know Your plan for me is good. To bring me to my expected end. You're like a good, good Father. You love me with no restraints. You are forever reaching for me. And for that, I'm thankful. You will never leave me nor forsake me. You will go with me even until the end. Amen.

Do you have some challenging circumstances that make you question life?
Is God really faithful and true? Sometimes life will make you ponder on this.
Write about some things you are thankful for, even the hard ones.

Day 14

And for that the dream was doubled unto Pharaoh twice; it is because the thing is established by God, and God will shortly bring it to pass.

Genesis 41:32

Dreams were patterns that God used repeatedly. He used one dream to speak to Joseph about Mary, and another time, he warned him to take Mary and flee from Bethlehem. Daniel had dreams of prophecy and interpreted dreams. Joseph, son of Jacob, had dreams in his younger years that he would rule over his brothers. The Lord sent angels many times in dreams to speak into situations.

The Bible speaks of people seeing visions and dreaming dreams as warnings. Sometimes, it is about the future. Sometimes, about the present. We can see that God used dreams to speak into people's lives. Today's scripture shows that Pharaoh had the dream twice because it was established by God and would come to pass. If you are a dreamer, you can relate to these patterns. I have had dreams that I know were from God. We can all ask God to allow us to dream for clarification. Whether you are a dreamer or not, God can use other people's dreams to give you an answer.

Prayer (speak aloud)

God, I ask You to let me dream for the present and future. I need guidance in my life. You spoke to many prophets through dreams. I am not Daniel or Joseph. I may never have a dream that would save a whole nation, but Your Word says that I could desire good gifts. I hope you use the pattern of dreams today to help me on my journey. Lord, You can allow someone else to dream about me. They can release a word for my situation. I'm willing to be used by You in this area. God, You're the same yesterday, today, and forever. Your Word is an example for me to live by. You used dreams as an avenue to speak to others. I'm open, God, for what You have for me. Amen.

Are you a dreamer? Does God speak to you through dreams? Do you see how God uses dreams in patterns?

_____

_____

_____

_____

_____

_____

_____

_____

_____

_____

_____

_____

_____

_____

_____

_____

_____

_____

_____

_____

_____

_____

_____

Day 15

Give, and it shall be given unto you; good measure, pressed down, and shaken together, and running over, shall men give into your bosom. For with the same measure that ye mete withal it shall be measured to you again.

Luke 6:38

Giving has always been a key pattern. Whether we give finances, prayer, or time, it will always return to us. Sowing and reaping is a staple throughout the Bible. I love this scripture because we can see the principle, the pattern, and the promise play out in one verse. When we give, we open up the future to give back to us. If we sow sparingly, we reap sparingly. If we sow abundantly, we will reap abundantly. God has always used the pattern of men giving back to you. All blessings come from God, through men to men.

It's not only a financial plan. We can sow into our own lives with self-care. We must take care of these temples. When we abuse our bodies, the outcome is not good. If we eat a lot of unhealthy foods, it will show up in our bodies eventually. If we don't grow in wisdom, it will show up in our decisions. We can see how sowing, no matter the form, will bring a harvest. Your harvest will show what you have sown. So give the best no matter what and reap the best harvest. The same measure you give out will be the measure you gain. Sow well.

Prayer (speak aloud)

Dear Father, I will sow my best, whether small or big. Please help me to grow in this pattern. Please show me how, when, and how much to give. Help me to sow good seeds. I will help my brothers and sisters struggling with life's stormy sea. Lead me to the ones I'm supposed to sow into. God, You didn't leave me without a remedy in these hard seasons. I will give of myself. I will take care of the body that You entrusted me with. Teach me to sow into others the way I would want someone to sow into me. I know the measure I mete out will be measured back to me. I want Your blessing to be shaken together and running over. I know others will give unto my bosom. Amen.

Do you practice this pattern? Do you give consistently?
Will you give something today?
Money, time, and a kind word can easily be a seed.

Day 16

And be not conformed to this world: but
be ye transformed by the renewing of your
mind, that ye may prove what is that good,
and acceptable, and perfect, will of God.

Romans 12:2

The Lord speaks about the mind throughout His Word. We can see why it's such an important subject. We often hear that every battle is won or lost in the mind. The pattern in this scripture is renewing our minds. Even when we give our lives to God, our minds are not automatically saved. We have to grow in this area. As babies in Christ, we don't know what we don't know. As we grow, we learn from our church leaders. We learn as we read the Bible, reading and meditating on the scriptures. It takes time to transform our minds.

It can be a challenge to turn around the thoughts we had before coming to God. That is why renewing the mind falls into the pattern category. The word renew is a repeated action. We renew our car tags yearly. People will renew their wedding vows occasionally. We renew subscriptions to medicines, glasses, etc. Let's renew our minds daily by feeding on the Word of God. When we renew our minds using this pattern, we will prove what is the good, acceptable, and perfect will of God.

Prayer (speak aloud)

God, please touch my mind even now. Please help me grow in this area and help me understand what I must do. You gave me my mind. You also gave me free will to think about what and how I want to. Sometimes, God, I wish You didn't give me that freedom. It would be easier to always think about the right things. I can see why the choice has been put in my hands. You want me to love You from my heart and not be forced. You want me to renew my mind because that is what my heart desires. I can clearly see the pattern in this scripture. I want to be obedient to Your patterns so that my life will reflect Your image. I pray that I can help others to grow in this area. Amen.

**What are some things that you do to keep
your mind renewed?
Was it hard for you to change the way you thought?
Journal today about your journey to renewing your mind.**

_____
_____
_____
_____
_____
_____
_____
_____
_____
_____
_____
_____
_____
_____
_____
_____
_____
_____
_____
_____
_____
_____

Day 17

And when he had sent the multitudes away,
he went up into a mountain apart to pray:
and when the evening was come, he was
there alone.

Matthew 14:23

Matthew, Mark, Luke, and John all recorded Jesus going away to pray. Jesus not only told us to pray, He showed us that it was a necessity. The Gospels show the pattern that Jesus often followed. Going away, going up, and being alone. We don't go up to the mountains to pray. I believe it's symbolic of us going to that place in our minds. Rising above the noise and all the obligations that we face daily. Getting alone so that we can pour our hearts out to God. It may be in our prayer closet or wherever works for you.

The main insight in this reflection is to see the pattern of prayer in our lives. Jesus prayed often. He set an example for us. Many times, after a great feat, Jesus would pull away from the crowd. He would seek to be alone. Maybe because the people wanted to make Him an object of worship. We worship Him today because of the price He paid for us. At that time, He wanted them to glorify the Father more than Him. Maybe He needed to pray to ensure His heart stayed in the right place. After all, He was flesh. The Bible says He was tempted in all points like we are, yet without sin. Jesus felt the need to pray always. Let's follow His lead.

Prayer (speak aloud)

Heavenly Father, I thank You for the example You gave us in the pattern of prayer. I will get away from the crowd. I will find that place of solitude. I will go up to the mountain (a place away from the noise) and pray. You left us a perfect example through Your son, Jesus Christ. He went often. He went early. He went alone. I know that if my Savior had to have a prayer life, I'd be doomed without one. Thank You for the opportunity to pray. What a great pattern to bring me to my purpose. You knew I would need this avenue to stay on the path You put me on. Without prayer, I would be like a ball in a pinball machine all over the place. I don't want to be that ball, sometimes winning and sometimes losing. With prayer, no matter the outcome, I'm a winner. Amen.

Is prayer an area you struggle with? I believe we all struggle in this area to some extent. Use these journal pages to write out your prayers.
I journal prayers almost daily. It helps me stay focused.

_____

_____

_____

_____

_____

_____

_____

_____

_____

_____

_____

_____

_____

_____

_____

_____

_____

_____

_____

_____

_____

_____

_____
_____
_____
_____
_____
_____
_____
_____
_____
_____
_____
_____
_____
_____
_____
_____
_____
_____
_____
_____

Day 18

And on the seventh day God ended his work
which he had made; and he rested on the
seventh day from all his work which he had
made. And God blessed the seventh day,
and sanctified it: because that in it he had
rested from all his work which God created
and made.

Genesis 2:2-3

Numbers have always been an important part of patterns. I chose these scriptures because the Bible introduces us to numbers early. I won't attempt to address each time numbers are referenced because that could be a whole Bible study by itself. What I want to exemplify is the patterns of numbers that are often found in scripture. Seven, three, and twelve are just a few that come to mind.

For six days, God worked (creating everything), and on the seventh day, he rested. On the third day, He rose up from the grave. He chose twelve disciples. Jacob had twelve sons, which became the twelve tribes of Israel. Jacob worked seven years for Rachel (or so he thought). He ended up with Leah and worked another seven years to finally have the one he really loved.

Let's not forget the forty. Jesus fasted for forty days. The children of Israel wandered in the wilderness for forty years. Moses's journey was broken up into forty years: forty years in Pharaoh's house, forty years in the desert as a shepherd, and forty years in the wilderness as a leader. The pattern of numbers is another language God uses to help us in the different seasons of our lives.

Prayer (speak aloud)

God, You are so good to us. You gave us patterns throughout Your Word. I know that numbers are one of the top patterns that You have chosen. I thank You for these patterns because I can go to Your Word in a hard season and see I have hope in the timing. You always came at the right time for many of our forefathers. I know that if I hold on to You no matter the situation, You will come to my rescue. I may have to fast for three days or sacrifice for twenty-one days to see things come to pass. I ask You to lead me in this area of times, seasons, and patterns. Let me know when to hold on and when to let go. I know that even now, I'm in a season that is running into years. At each significant number, I'm always hopeful and expecting a change. It's not always easy to wait for the season to change. I'm thankful that You always let me know You are with me. You're the same yesterday, today, and forever. I will wait like Job until my change comes. Amen.

What is your favorite number in the Bible? What is a story that you stand on while you're waiting?
I love seven and three.

_____

_____

_____

_____

_____

_____

_____

_____

_____

_____

_____

_____

_____

_____

_____

_____

_____

_____

_____

_____

_____

Day 19

And Elijah said unto her, Fear not; go and do as thou hast said: but make me thereof a little cake first, and bring it unto me, and after make for thee and for thy son. And she went and did according to the saying of Elijah: and she, and he, and her house, did eat many days.

1 Kings 17:13,15

Most are familiar with Elijah and the widow from Zarephath. If you are not, take a minute and read the story in this chapter. The pattern I want to highlight is how God often used the prophets to speak into people's lives. He often gave warnings, instructions, and encouragement through His Prophets. As we can see, it could mean life or death for those in the Bible. It's a pattern woven throughout the Bible and the Church world today.

When Jesus came, he made it possible for all of us at any given time to go to Him for our needs or answers to prayer. God also intended for pastors to be a voice in our lives. Yes, I already know that not all pastors are led by God. That is why we must have our spiritual discernment intact. But that doesn't cancel out God's pattern. Mankind will fail us; that's a given. Ask God to help you know when a person is speaking into your life, whether they are of God or not. The pattern is that Elijah's instructions saved not only the widow but her son as well. It may seem counterintuitive, but it could mean death or life.

Prayer (speak aloud)

God, this one can be a hard pattern to follow. Please help me be sensitive to Your spirit and know when the person who is giving me instructions or advice is the one You sent. The pattern has been set for my own protection. I'm thankful that I can pray, and You will answer. I'm grateful I don't have to go to a priest for God to hear me. I know that when You put something in the Bible that shows up repeatedly, it's a sure sign that it's for my good. I know that You have put pastors, prophets, and people of God to speak into my life. Sometimes, I can't hear from You because of my pain or the noise drowning out Your voice. Thank You for the examples of patterns that will keep me and, many times, keep my family. Amen.

**Do you have someone you trust to speak over your life?
Have you ever considered the importance of this pattern?**

_____

_____

_____

_____

_____

_____

_____

_____

_____

_____

_____

_____

_____

_____

_____

_____

_____

_____

_____

_____

_____

_____

_____

_____

Day 20

And he said, Take now thy son, thine only
son Isaac, whom thou lovest, and get thee
into the land of Moriah; and offer him there
for a burnt offering upon one of the mountains which I will tell thee of.

Genesis 22:2

Sacrifice can easily be seen in the 3 P's. The pattern that we want to reveal is that God requires sacrifice in our lives. We often think of Abraham when we hear about sacrifice. In this verse, it's referred to as a burnt offering. In Biblical days, something had to die. Thank God Jesus made the ultimate sacrifice for us. The key is laying down our agenda for God's agenda. Not our will, but His. How do we do this?

We don't kill animals or, God forbid, our children. Romans 12:1 states that we should present our bodies as living sacrifices. What does that look like nowadays? Pray daily. Fast often. Prefer others' wants above your own. Be faithful to your church. Be faithful with your giving. The Bible encourages us to be givers. Giving, whether it's money, time, or help, is one of the most significant sacrifices. Our daily lives should reflect a pattern of sacrifices. Sacrifices can be found in being still and not running ahead of God. Don't undervalue your commitment to listening to God when making decisions. It's a great sacrifice/offering to God to be still when others run ahead of you. In Paul's words, we die daily.

Prayer (speak aloud)

God, I thank You for redeeming me with the blood of Your son Jesus Christ. Thank You for the examples throughout Your Word that show me the patterns. Thank You that I don't have to sacrifice an animal every day. I often laugh to myself, thinking of what my backyard would look like if I had to kill something for my sins. I will gladly die daily in my walk with You. I will give when You tell me to. I will give my time in prayer. Help me to be Your hands and feet everywhere I go. Please give me the strength to be still when the world around me is pushing on me. Give me the ear to hear that still, small voice. I want to present my body and life as a living sacrifice for Your Kingdom. Amen.

What is something that you do for God that You feel is a sacrifice?
What does it look like for you to die daily, like Paul?
Thank God Jesus paid the debt we couldn't pay.

_____

_____

_____

_____

_____

_____

_____

_____

_____

_____

_____

_____

_____

_____

_____

_____

_____

_____

_____

_____

_____

_____

Part 3
Promises

Day 21

**For all the promises of God in him are
yea, and in him Amen, unto the glory of
God by us.**

2 Corinthians 1:20

I started with this verse because I want you to know that God doesn't backtrack on His promises. His promises are yea and amen. The reality is that most of His promises are conditional. If you will, He will.

Let's look at some of His promises that are staples for the church. He will always be with us. He will never leave us or forsake us. Consider the lilies. They neither toil nor spin, yet God says that not even Solomon, in all his glory, was arrayed like one of them. Don't be anxious about what you will eat or drink. Don't worry about your provision. Seek Him first, and all these things will be added to you. We see a principle in this as well as a pattern. When God lays out a pattern, the promise is sure to follow. Beauty for ashes. The oil of joy for mourning. A garment of praise for the spirit of heaviness that we might be called the trees of righteousness. What a trade! We give Him our brokenness, and He promises to make us whole. No matter what your life may lack, when you bring it to God, He will make up the difference. Let's stand on His Word that His promises are way better than what we can offer Him.

Prayer (speak aloud)

Thank You, Heavenly Father, for all the promises in the Bible. One promise that I cling to is that You love me. You love me with an everlasting love. Your love for me is unconditional. I know You don't love the sin that is in my life sometimes. You have given me the most wonderful promise of trading my broken life for a whole, healed life. I'm thankful for the assurance of Your provision. You are a faithful God. You are good to me even when I'm not good. Mercy is a promise. Forgiveness is a promise. Salvation is promised to me if I turn from my old ways, my sins. I don't know what makes You want to keep going beyond for me. I'm weak in my flesh most days. Your promises are so much greater than I deserve. For that, I'm thankful. Amen.

What are some of your favorite promises in the Bible? Journal about some promises that have manifested in your life.

_____

_____

_____

_____

_____

_____

_____

_____

_____

_____

_____

_____

_____

_____

_____

_____

_____

_____

_____

_____

_____

Day 22

The steps of a good man are ordered by the LORD: and he delighteth in his way. Though he fall, he shall not be utterly cast down: for the LORD upholdeth him with his hand.

Psalm 37:23-24

Bibleinfo.com says that in one account, there are 3,573 promises in the Bible. The word "promise" is found 50 times in the KJV. I won't claim to know that these numbers are accurate. I'm sure I won't even touch the tip of the iceberg in these last eleven days. My goal is to encourage you with the ones we all stand on.

What better passage than these to expound on the promises of God. Our steps are ordered by the Lord. We delighteth in the ways of God. The key in verse 23 is a good man. We all know that our flesh is not good. The good man is the one who seeks after the things of God. His spirit is always towards God. God delights in us when we put him first. We will fall from time to time. God will uphold us with His hand. What a promise! We will not utterly be cast down. The promise in this passage lets us know that God is going before us. He will guide us to the right path. He will lead us in the right direction. The people we are supposed to meet will be there. The door that needs to be closed will be closed. The door that we need to open, God will open.

Prayer (speak aloud)

Dear God, guide my steps. Lead me in the path that You set up for me. I know that I fall from time to time. I don't always make the best decisions. You promised to help me. No matter what my day consists of, I need You. I am so thankful for Your nudges, love, and mercy. Thank You for ordering my steps. You close doors that no man can open. You open doors no man can shut. You make a way out of no way. You make streams in the desert. You bring the right person at the right time. If I need strength, You bring joy. If my family is in need, You supply that need. You keep Your promises. Amen.

Have you ever experienced God ordering your steps? Journal about some times that God went before you.

_____
_____
_____
_____
_____
_____
_____
_____
_____
_____
_____
_____
_____
_____
_____
_____
_____
_____
_____
_____

Day 23

Now after the death of Moses the servant of the LORD it came to pass, that the LORD spake unto Joshua the son of Nun, Moses' minister, saying, Moses my servant is dead; now therefore arise, go over this Jordan, thou, and all this people, unto the land which I do give to them, even to the children of Israel. Every place that the sole of your foot shall tread upon, that have I given unto you, as I said unto Moses.

Joshua 1:1-3

Joshua Chapter 1 is one of my favorite chapters in the Bible. Promise after promise is woven throughout this chapter. Moses has died. The Lord is speaking to Joshua to go forward and take the children of Israel into the Promised Land. He promised Joshua that every place he put his foot would be given unto him. What an incredible feat that had been passed on to Joshua. It wasn't just laid in his lap. There was work to do and battles to be fought. God commanded him to be strong and courageous.

As we read further in this chapter, we see that there are more unique strategies that would cause them to prosper and succeed in their endeavors. Don't turn the right hand or the left means to stay focused on God. Meditate upon the Word day and night. Because the Word is a two-edged sword, we can fight battles and never even have to engage physically. When you know the promises of God, you won't worry about the enemy. God promises to defeat the enemy for us. He was defeated on the cross. Knowing God's Word will be one of the greatest weapons you will ever use. God promises to be with us in every situation.

Prayer (speak aloud)

Dear God, a lot of my forefathers are gone. I know that the paton has been passed on to me. Thank You, God, for all the promises that You have given me to win this race. Whenever I read these stories, it builds my faith. My hope grows stronger. Thank You for these examples, which tell me that You will keep Your promises. Your Word says my life is in Your hands. You will send angels to watch over me and my loved ones. Thank You for allowing me to be victorious. Your Word is my treasure chest of promises. I will meditate on Your Word day and night. I will praise You even in the difficult seasons. You promised joy would come in the morning. You're fighting for me even when I'm sleeping. What great comfort that is to me! Amen.

What stands out to you in this reflection?
Do you feel like God has a job for you to do?
What are some actions you will take to move you forward?

Day 24

**Thou wilt keep him in perfect peace,
whose mind is stayed on thee: because
he trusteth in thee.**

Isaiah 26:3

I don't know about you, but if we ever needed the peace of God in our lives, it is now. We see that each promise comes with stipulations. There may be some that we don't have to do anything. For example, His love for us is unconditional. But, for the most part, we must do our part to see the promises of God manifest in our lives.

Peace is something we all long for. Our mind is like a garden. Whatever we plant will grow. This is why it's so important that we pay attention to what we allow our minds to dwell on. Thoughts are seeds. You have a promise from God in this scripture that peace can be your harvest. It will not just happen. We must be intentional about what we read, watch, or even think about. God will keep those in perfect peace whose minds stay on Him. I'm not against medicine. The Bible refers to a merry heart doeth good like a medicine. It can help, no doubt. But, if we are not careful, we will look to man to bring us peace through a pill. The Bible also lets us know that the Word of God is also a healer. It will heal our minds and bring peace to our chaos. What a trade. What a promise. Let's get our minds on God and His Word. Peace will surely follow.

Prayer (speak aloud)

Thank You, God, for the remedy to have peace in my life. I will keep my mind stayed on thee. Your Word is my peace. Through that peace, I have learned to trust the process. Thank You for perfect peace. Thank You for peace of mind. You promise to perfect the things that concern me. I will meditate upon Your Word day and night. Oh, how glad I am to know about Your promises. Thank You for being so patient and merciful to me as I grow in Your Kingdom. Your love and compassion shine through each day. This peace of God is contagious. Please help me let the peace dwelling in my life overflow into others. I will share this great promise that I have in You. Amen.

**Do you have a hard time keeping peace in your mind?
What is something you can do to help yourself in this area?
One of Satan's greatest weapons against us is our mind.**

_____
_____
_____
_____
_____
_____
_____
_____
_____
_____
_____
_____
_____
_____
_____
_____
_____
_____
_____
_____
_____
_____
_____
_____

Day 25

For I know the thoughts that I think toward you, saith the LORD, thoughts of peace, and not of evil, to give you an expected end.

Jeremiah 29:11

This scripture has undoubtedly appeared in several of the Bee Devotionals. It's a multifaceted verse laced with comfort and the knowledge that God cares deeply about us. His thoughts toward us are of peace, not evil, to give us an expected end. We could stop right here and praise him for hours. What a promise!

Psalms 139:18 says His thoughts toward us are more than the sand. Whether we are sleeping or awake, He is thinking about us. The beautiful promise in this verse is He wants to give us our heart's desire. What are you expecting today from God? We can all be happy knowing that He wants the best for us. I read a quote several years ago that says, "He is not mad at us. He is mad about us." We are deeply flawed. Yet, we are deeply loved. What a trade. What a promise. God wants to see His plan fulfilled in your life. It's His good pleasure to bless us. He compares His desires for us to what we desire for our children or loved ones. We want the best for them. We will help them if it is in our power to do so. We will love them no matter how far they wander away from the church. That's how God sees us.

Prayer (speak aloud)

God, I know that I break Your heart sometimes. I know that I sometimes make the wrong choices. I don't always say the right things. Thank You for not disowning me when my flesh tries to rule. My faith stays strong, knowing that You want the best for me. I can have peace knowing that You are working on my behalf. Thank You for always working behind the scenes for my good. You made a way for me to have perfect peace. Your Word is my lifeline. It's my strength when I'm weak. It's my bread when my soul is hungry. It's my drink when I'm thirsty. Knowing You have made all things possible if I simply hold on to Your promises is a great comfort. Amen.

Do you love Jeremiah 29:11?
What do you love the most about it?
It's one of my favorites.

_____
_____
_____
_____
_____
_____
_____
_____
_____
_____
_____
_____
_____
_____
_____
_____
_____
_____
_____
_____
_____

Day 26

God is not a man, that he should lie; Neither the son of man, that he should repent: Hath he said, and shall he not do it? Or hath he spoken, and shall he not make it good?

Numbers 23:19

Man will let you down. Man will lie to you. Man will deceive you. God will not. One thing you can count on is God will always speak the truth to you. Whatever God says, you can take it to the bank. You can put it in your account and withdraw from it without worrying about insufficient funds. His promises will stand forever. If God said He would do it, don't settle for anything less.

What a powerful scripture that we are reading today. Hath He said, and shall not do it? Makes me want to shout right now. Hath He spoken it, and shall He not make it good. I have found that God's timing is not our timing. Abraham waited 25 years for his promised child. It was 22 years before Joseph would see his dream come to pass. Moses was 80 when he stepped into being the deliverer God called him to be from his mother's womb. I have promises that I have been waiting on for over ten years. Is it easy? Not really. Verses like this help me to stay encouraged and focused on the future. God will make it happen when it's time.

Prayer (speak aloud)

God, You are so faithful to Your people. You have never lied to me, and You never will. My heart gets heavy in the wait sometimes. I find myself losing hope. Then I read Your Word, and I get a second wind. I feed my spirit with Your Word, and I'm encouraged to keep holding on. You will make good what You have spoken. Thank You for helping me make it through the hard days. You always give me a little refresher while I wait. If I wait on You, I can mount up like an eagle. I will run and not grow weary. I will walk and not faint. I will hold on to Your promises. Amen.

Are you waiting for a promise to come to pass?
I encourage you not to settle; keep believing.
Journal about the season you are in.

_____

_____

_____

_____

_____

_____

_____

_____

_____

_____

_____

_____

_____

_____

_____

_____

_____

_____

_____

_____

_____

_____

_____

_____

Day 27

And we know that all things work together
for good to them that love God, to them who
are the called according to his purpose.

Romans 8:28

"Every believer has quoted this scripture at least once. It is a staple in the Christian's life." When life throws us curve balls, we stand by this promise. I can clearly see the 3 P's in this scripture. Knowing that God is working all things for our good is undeniably the greatest truth we can put in our quiver.

I have used this verse a few times in my other devotionals because there are many insights you can draw from it. I often say that we get this verse twisted and misquote it. We say all things are good, but that is not the case usually. More often than not, life is acting crazy. Our hearts are getting broken. Darkness surrounds us almost daily. Death is constantly reminding us that life is short. We are called according to His purpose. We are not doing our own thing, or we shouldn't be. When we are looking to Him, depending on Him, and praying, He is working on our behalf. The good, the bad, and yes, even the ugly will be worked out for good when we put all our trust in Him. What a promise!

Prayer (speak aloud)

Dear God, thank You for always having my best interest in mind. Thank You for scriptures like this that help me get through the hard days. You are always with me. You love me and keep me on my journey. Thank You for working all things for my good. I love You, which means I'm being obedient. When Satan comes knocking, I will let You answer that door. When finances are tight, You are there. During the good days and the hard days, You are always going before me. You called me to work with purpose. You called me to be a soul winner. You have shown me that you work on my behalf, even when life gets hard. You got me. I trust You. Amen.

How many times have you stood on this scripture when you got punched in the gut by life? Meditate on one of those times and write about your experience.

_____

_____

_____

_____

_____

_____

_____

_____

_____

_____

_____

_____

_____

_____

_____

_____

_____

_____

_____

_____

_____

_____

_____

_____

Day 28

**He that dwelleth in the secret place of the
Most High Shall abide under the shadow of
the Almighty.**

Psalm 91:1

I don't have the room to put the whole chapter of Psalm 91. We all have quoted this chapter over and over. Many promises are listed in these 16 verses. It is, without a doubt, one of my favorite chapters in the whole Bible. Why? The promises written in this chapter alone can keep us for the rest of our lives. When we call on Him, He will answer. He gives His angels charge over us. They protect us. They go before us. We don't have to be afraid of the enemy. A thousand shall fall at our side and ten thousand at our right hand. No evil shall befall us. No plague shall come near our dwelling. With a long life, He satisfies us. We don't have to fear the terror by night or the arrows by day. We don't have to be afraid of the darkness. God is the light. He protects us. We need only to abide under the shadow of the almighty. Thank God for the promises.

Prayer (speak aloud)

God, You are so mindful of me. I don't deserve these kinds of promises. In this chapter, You have given me a list of promises to keep me going throughout my life. There have been many times that I deserved death. Yet You came to my rescue with life. Thank You for Your protection. Thank You for Your provision. Thank You for loving me even in my undeserving times. How wonderful You are to keep helping me. I always look to this chapter in Psalms to strengthen my journey. I don't have to be afraid when the enemy throws his best shot. I simply speak Your Word. Your Word is in my heart. Your Word is my weapon. It's my light in the darkness. You have promised to never leave me nor forsake me. Amen.

Do you quote Psalm 91 when you're in battle?
Please take a minute and read it today.
Write out the whole chapter. It will encourage you.

Day 29

**These things I have spoken unto you, that
in me ye might have peace. In the world ye
shall have tribulation: but be of good cheer;
I have overcome the world.**

John 16:33

Trouble, tribulation, and chaos are knocking on our doors daily. Without knowing the promises of God, we could easily be afraid. Even as I write this devotional, we are days away from the 2024 presidential election. Fear is driving people to panic and stockpile supplies. Fear is pushing many of God's children around. This should not be an issue in the Church. Yes, we will face unpleasant circumstances. We could see war in our country. I encourage you today to put His Word in your heart. Take it to heart. Be of good cheer. He has overcome the world. He will give us perfect peace. We must remember to keep our minds upon Him. He is the living Word. He is our hope in a hopeless world. He is the promise that we can hold on to. Draw close to Him, and He will draw close to you. The more you know His Word, the less afraid you will be when trouble comes.

Prayer (speak aloud)

Heavenly Father, I look to You to keep me in these uncertain times. I know that you have promised me peace. I can look to You for the courage to stand in the face of the tribulation. The tribulation will come. Weapons will form against me, but I have great consultation in Your Word that I will stand. I will not let fear drive me. Your Word says fear has torment. I will be of good cheer because You have overcome the world. God, You see all the things that are going on. People are fighting one another. They are killing one another. Fear is trying to keep Your people tied down. Please help me to help others through these devotionals to see a mighty God keep His promises. You gave me the road map to make it to Heaven. It's called the Holy Bible. Amen.

Do you get fearful when the world starts pushing its agenda? Write a prayer for where you are right now, and believe God will move.

_____

_____

_____

_____

_____

_____

_____

_____

_____

_____

_____

_____

_____

_____

_____

_____

_____

_____

_____

_____

_____

_____

Day 30

Fear thou not; for I am with thee: be not dismayed; for I am thy God: I will strengthen
thee; yea, I will help thee; yea, I will uphold
thee with the right hand of my righteousness.

Isaiah 41:10

This verse lists seven promises: Fear not. He is with us. Don't be dismayed. He is God. He will strengthen us, help us, and uphold us with His righteous right hand. If we ever needed these promises, we need them now. The world is driving its agenda every day.

Fear is the strongest weapon that the enemy has in his arsenal. We must have our helmet of salvation on to protect our minds. When we know we are saved, we better understand how God feels about us. To know that everything He did was to save us from this wicked enemy, we can have bold faith. Fear has to take a back seat. He is our God, and we are His people. He promises to help us. He promises to lift us. The right hand is symbolic of power. Deuteronomy 28:7 says our enemies will come at us one way, but God will cause them to flee seven ways. The more we know His promises, the less we will fear. The strength that we receive will help us keep fighting. Knowing that God is helping us will keep us encouraged. He is a way maker, promise keeper, and light in the darkness.

Prayer (speak aloud):

Thank You, God, for the promises throughout Your Word. You didn't leave us without hope. I won't fear or be dismayed. You are God and God alone. Thank You for keeping me day to day. Thank You for giving me strength in my physical body. Thank You for peace when the world is in chaos. You're a good, good Father. You promised to hear our prayers. I know that there is a prayer bowl in Heaven. Long after I am gone from this ole world, my prayers will still be active in the spirit. I can rest assured that You will visit my lost children. You compared Your love for me to how I love my own children. I won't give them a stone if they ask for bread. I won't ignore their cry for help. You won't ignore my heartfelt cries. How can I not be strengthened in my spiritual man? Amen.

129

**List these seven promises.
Beside each promise, share a time that they manifested in
your life.**

_____

_____

_____

_____

_____

_____

_____

_____

_____

_____

_____

_____

_____

_____

_____

_____

_____

_____

_____

_____

_____

Day 31

And Moses said unto the people, Fear ye
not, stand still, and see the salvation of the
Lᴏʀᴅ, which he will shew to you to day: for
the Egyptians whom ye have seen to day, ye
shall see them again no more for ever. The
Lᴏʀᴅ shall fight for you, and ye shall hold
your peace.

Exodus 14:13-14

I see a common thread in these passages about God's promises: fear. We have already referred to it several times in this devotional. Let's take this promise section all the way home because we know we already win. How do we know that we have won? Because God promises to fight for us.

We make it harder than it has to be. We get in God's way, trying to fight Satan with our own thinking. We worry. We get overwhelmed. We get fearful. God says in this scripture to hold our peace. In verse 13, God says the Egyptians you see today, you will see no more. What a promise. I have probably mentioned Hosea 4:6 in every devotional. My people are destroyed for lack of knowledge. When we don't know the promises, we will forfeit our peace. We will forfeit our hopes, dreams, and desires to see better days. Let's hold on to God's promises. Let's stand on the Word. Let's hold our peace and let God fight our battles. Let God be God.

Prayer (speak aloud):

God, Your promises are woven all through the Bible. I will not waver from the knowledge You have allowed me to consume. I understand that Your promises are yes and amen. Thank You for fighting unseen battles. For going before me. Protecting me. Keeping me. Helping me. You cannot fail. It is hard not to worry. Philippians 4:6 is my go-to verse. I won't be anxious. I will be thankful, pray, and bring my supplication to You. Your promises will sustain me till my days on this earth have ended. You have given me all things that pertain to life and godliness. You promise to work all things for my good. Your Word is the promise. You are faithful in forgiving me when I fall short of Your expectations of me. Thank You for Your principles, patterns, and promises. Amen.

Take a few minutes and use the last few journal pages to
share what stood out most in this devotional.
Which section was your favorite? Why?

_____

_____

_____

_____

_____

_____

_____

_____

_____

_____

_____

_____

_____

_____

_____

_____

_____

_____

_____

_____

_____

_____

_____

Why bees?

My series of Bee Devotionals was birthed out of a deep desire to have a ministry that would encourage, inspire, and pour into somebody else who wants to make a difference. Don't let what others say about you or even your own thinking limit a limitless God. The bumblebee shouldn't be able to fly because of the structure of its body, but it flies anyway. So can you.

Over the next few years, I'm hoping to develop a total of 12 "How to Be…" devotionals to inspire and encourage Christians who want more out of life. Recently, I set up my website, beeministries.com, where you can find out more and read my blog. My YouTube channel for Bee Ministries offers devotional readings, sermons, heartfelt stories, and inspirational words. My first book, Life After the Mistake, is a creative nonfiction story about what it's like to be caught up in the sin of adultery. It's available on Amazon along with the Bee Devotional series and a short ebook I developed called How to Bee a Writer.

From the bottom of my heart, thank you for reading my book and taking the time to let God work within you through words. It changed me. And I believe it can change you too.

-Sheila

MORE BOOKS BY SHEILA TEXTOR

Introducing Victory

She is strong. She is vibrant.

I can't take credit for her beauty or her strong personality. I needed my own signature bee (her creator is listed on the copyright page). She flourishes throughout each new devotional. She flies around the journal pages to keep you focused on your own thoughts for that day. She carries the promises of the word through the daily reflections. She is my sweet Victory!

She is vibrant, she is positive, she is Victory!

NEED MORE SPACE TO JOURNAL?

ALL BOOKS AVAILABLE ON AMAZON

Made in the USA
Middletown, DE
15 November 2025